Careers in
ENGINEERING

A Career in Computer Engineering

Careers in ENGINEERING

A Career in Computer Engineering

Stuart A. Kallen

ReferencePoint Press®

San Diego, CA

For more information, contact:
ReferencePoint Press, Inc.
PO Box 27779
San Diego, CA 92198
www.ReferencePointPress.com

Picture credits:
cover: bjdlzx/iStockphoto.com
6: Maury Aaseng
11: wavebreakmedia/Shutterstock.com
20: Laura A. Oda/MCT/Newscom
28: dotshock/Shutterstock.com
42: GaudiLab/Shutterstock.com

LIBRARY OF CONGRESS CATALOGING-IN-PUBLICATION DATA

Name: Kallen, Stuart A., 1955, author.
Title: A Career in Computer Engineering/by Stuart A. Kallen.
Description: San Diego, CA: ReferencePoint Press, Inc., 2019. | Series: Careers in Engineering |
    Includes bibliographical references and index. | Audience: Grades 9 to 12.
Identifiers: LCCN 2018021278 (print) | LCCN 2018022000 (ebook) | ISBN 9781682823484 (eBook) |
    ISBN 9781682823477 (hardback)
Subjects: LCSH: Computer engineering—Vocational guidance—Juvenile literature.
Classification: LCC TK7885.5 (ebook) | LCC TK7885.5 .K35 2019 (print) | DDC 621.39023—dc23
LC record available at https://lccn.loc.gov/2018021278

CONTENTS

COMPUTER ENGINEER AT A GLANCE

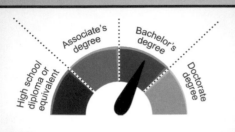

Educational Requirements

High school diploma or equivalent · Associate's degree · Bachelor's degree · Doctorate degree

Certification and Licensing

Professional engineer license (voluntary)

Working Conditions

Indoors

Personal Qualities

- ✓ Creative
- ✓ Strong math and science abilities
- ✓ Technical expertise
- ✓ Communication skills
- ✓ Team player

Median annual pay in 2016 $115,080

73,600

Number of jobs as of 2016

Growth rate through 2026 *5%*

Future Job Outlook

Source: Bureau of Labor Statistics, *Occupational Outlook Handbook*. www.bls.gov.

Engineers Make It Work

Every day countless people dream of founding a successful technology company like Apple or Microsoft. These visionaries might go as far to imagine a company founded on a game-changing product and even pencil out the money they hope to make from their unique idea. But every tech dreamer who would like to start a company would do well to follow the advice of Apple cofounder Steve Wozniak: "We have ideas for companies, ideas for revenues and products. [But] don't forget to include the engineers—they are trained to solve problems. That's what they're really good at."[1] There are few careers as versatile as engineering, and engineers rely on multiple talents and skills to solve problems. Engineers use their knowledge of math, science, analysis, and design—and even art—to produce new machines, materials, systems, and structures. They spend their days identifying problems to solve, proposing various solutions, testing concepts, and investigating data.

Wozniak, affectionately known as Woz, is a computer scientist and electrical engineer. He invented the first Apple computers that launched the personal computing revolution in the late 1970s. Wozniak understands that a clever idea or a new approach to marketing a product is not enough to achieve success. Engineers are needed to turn an idea into reality: "Does it work? For engineering, everything has to work."[2] says Wozniak.

An Exciting and Promising Field

Perhaps no specialty has transformed society more profoundly than computer engineering, which is a subdiscipline of electrical engineering. Computers have changed the way people communicate, learn, shop, travel, play games, make music, watch movies, and even exercise. And computer engineers are the masterminds behind the digital revolution. These professionals design, test, construct, and maintain computers and computer-controlled equipment.

The work of computer engineers can be seen in laptop, desktop, and tablet computers. Computer engineers also design workstations, printers, modems, network servers, smartphones, and supercomputers. In addition they are creators of the internal hardware elements that make computers function smoothly and efficiently. These components include motherboards, memory chips, processors, video cards, hard drives, and power supplies. Computer engineers embed computers in cars, airplanes, appliances, and other machines. They build hardware for communications networks and labor to make computers faster, smaller, and smarter.

> "The opportunity to have an original impact through building important and specialized [computers] is larger than anything I've seen before."[3]
>
> —MIT engineering professor Joel Emer

The work of computer engineers produces industrial computer systems used for manufacturing, energy production, agriculture, and other businesses. If a device has any digital functions, a computer hardware engineer helped design and test it. The work also requires computer engineers to have a thorough knowledge of computer software, and most are experts at writing computer code. They work with operating systems, applications, utilities, and security programs.

Computer engineers who focus on the future are working to incorporate digital functions into fabrics and building materials. Some are building hardware for the next generation of artificial intelligence, creating powerful computer hardware for driverless cars, drones, and spacecraft. Massachusetts Institute of Technology (MIT) professor Joel Emer is thrilled about the future of computer engineering: "I've been in this field for more than four decades. I've never seen an area with so much excitement and promise in all that time. The opportunity to have an original impact through building important and specialized [computer] architecture is larger than anything I've seen before."[3]

"Build Good Computers"

Most computer engineers work behind the scenes to innovate and create new products. But a few computer science pioneers went on to become well-known tech luminaries. Jeff Bezos trained as a computer engineer before starting the online retail site Amazon .com. Facebook cofounder Dustin Moskovitz, Twitter cofounder Jack Dorsey, and superstar computer games developer Markus Persson all began their careers as computer engineers.

And of course there is Woz, who as a teenager had a poster of a 1970s Cray supercomputer pinned on the wall of his bedroom. Like many pioneers, Wozniak's genius was not immediately recognized; his design for the Apple I computer was turned down by Hewlett-Packard on five occasions. Woz went on to found Apple with Steve Jobs who transformed the world with iPods, iPads, and iPhones. But unlike Jobs, Woz had no desire to conquer the tech world. As he stated in 2006, "My goal wasn't to make a ton of money. It was to build good computers. I only started the company when I realized I could be an engineer forever."[4] For those who dream of engineering computers forever, the field is practically unlimited during an era where computers are harvesting food, driving cars, and guiding rockets to Mars and beyond.

CHAPTER 1

What Does a Computer Engineer Do?

Computer engineers work with extremely complex equipment, and their job description can be equally complicated. Computer engineers apply their knowledge of electronics to computer hardware, computer systems engineering, and computer architecture (the basic construction and low-level programming of computers). Hardware engineers specialize in researching, developing, designing, and testing computer equipment that can range from pocket calculators to the giant servers used by social media and video streaming websites. Some invent and develop new equipment, while others update computers to make them faster and more efficient.

Computer systems engineers develop, test, and evaluate systems made up of computer circuits, microchips, and computer hardware components. They design internal hardware components, including data processors, graphics processing units (GPUs), and the central processing units (CPUs) that execute most of the commands from a computer's hardware and software. Computer engineer Dave Haynie explains his job: "I do system-level design . . . which means working out systems based on chips. . . . There are plenty of computer engineers who only design parts of very large systems, but I actually design whole computer systems."[5]

Other whole computer systems include information technology (IT) networks used by businesses and other organizations. Computer engineers who work in IT develop and manage systems made up of integrated components that manage operations, process financial accounts, control human resource information, and deliver digital products like e-books, music, movies, and games.

Computer engineers work in a variety of areas including hardware, systems engineering, and computer architecture. They might work with giant servers (pictured), tiny microchips, or other devices and technologies that enable computers to function.

While systems engineers work to create digital structures, other computer engineers focus on designing single chips, or even small parts of a chip. As Haynie says: "A buddy of mine . . . designed the DDR3 memory controller on the X-Box 360. That's a piece of a chip, of course, but a very critical one."[6]

Computer Engineering and Computer Science

The field of computer engineering significantly overlaps with that of computer science. Professionals in both fields understand the inner workings of computers and the software aspects of computer systems. What makes computer science unique is that the discipline originated in the 1970s at university math departments, whereas computer engineering grew out of electrical engineering departments. As a result computer science focuses on programming, computation, and algorithms (precise, step-by-step instructions that form the basis of computer programs). The difference between computer science and computer engineering is a matter of emphasis. Computer scientists work in theory and experimentation, while computer engineers are more likely to design, test, and build hardware.

Since computer engineers work with operating systems and software applications, they are experts in hardware-software integration. The smartphone industry provides a good example of this integration; new hardware and software is introduced simultaneously. This requires computer engineers to write, test, and analyze the software that will run on the devices they design. In this role computer engineers might develop software apps used for word processing, spreadsheets, database management, networking, utilities, and security. Computer engineers also write firmware, the computer programs that permanently control specific hardware in a device.

Computers Everywhere

The hardware components developed by computer engineers are used for information processing, communications, and storage. Products invented and produced by computer engineers can be found in a wide range of industries, including telecommunications, robotics, energy, health care, security, entertainment, gaming, and manufacturing.

Computer engineers are also behind the wide range of "smart" devices available to consumers. These gadgets, which include televisions, fitness trackers, refrigerators, home security systems, and even coffeepots, are embedded with complete computers built onto a single circuit board known as single board computers (SBCs). These small computing devices communicate to one another on a giant digital network called the Internet of Things (IoT) that is expected to drive the economy of the future. According to the research center McKinsey Global Institute, the IoT could be worth between $3.9 trillion and $11.1 trillion by 2025. By that time over 35 billion devices will be connected to the IoT. And computer engineers will be central to this development, as tech writer Daniel Burrus explains: "The Internet of Things revolves around increased machine-to-machine communication; it's built on cloud computing and networks of data-gathering sensors; it's mobile, virtual, and [allows] instantaneous connection."[7]

Some computer engineers work in the automotive field designing vehicles that can be described as computers on wheels. Every new car rolling off an assembly line has up to 150 embedded computer-controlled devices. Computer engineers design and test switches, sensors, drivers, microcontrollers, and other components in charge of everything from adjusting seats to regulating gas flow into the engine. Autonomous (self-driving) cars use even more complex digital systems. As automobile companies rush to develop autonomous cars, computer engineers are in great demand, according to computer engineer Sebastian Thrun: "It's not just the physical car but areas like navigation, LiDAR [long-range radar], cameras . . . so the need for [computer engineering] talent, both in hardware and software, is huge."[8]

> "It's not just the physical car but areas like navigation, LiDAR, cameras . . . so the need for [computer engineering] talent, both in hardware and software, is huge."[8]
>
> —Sebastian Thrun, computer engineer

Beyond typical consumer products, computer engineers design, test, and build industrial equipment in a field called computer-aided manufacturing (CAM). Those who work in CAM combine software with machinery that is used to automate manufacturing processes. CAM systems control all operations at a manufacturing plant, including production, transportation, management, and storage. Computers are central to CAM, which reduces waste, saves energy, increases production speeds, creates more consistent products, and efficiently tracks and orders materials. Industrial robots rely on embedded computers that program actions such as moving parts and materials, assembling products, and performing precise operations that are difficult or impossible for

Computers in Space

Outer space might be one of the most exciting new environments for computer engineering. In 2018 computer engineers at the University of Pittsburgh's NSF Center for Space, High-performance, and Resilient Computing (SHREC) launched one of the world's most powerful computers into orbit. The Space Test Program-Houston 6 (STP-H6) is a supercomputer built for the International Space Station (ISS), and it is three times more powerful than its predecessor. Computer engineers designed the STP-H6 with special shielding that allows the supercomputer to withstand galactic cosmic rays and other types of radiation found in the extreme environment of outer space. The computer will be used to perform numerous experiments while taking detailed pictures of Earth with its dual high-resolution cameras. SHREC founder Alan George explains: "Computer engineering for space is the ultimate challenge . . . since remote sensing [the scanning of the earth by satellite] and autonomous operation are the main purposes of spacecraft and both demand high-performance computing."

Quoted in Matt Cichowicz, "Engineering Team Develops Radiation-Resistant Computers Capable of High-Performance Computing in the Harshness of Space," Phys.org, March 6, 2018. https://phys.org.

humans. For example, robots are used at auto assembly plants to lift heavy car bodies and move them from one assembly line to another. Robots stamp out metal pieces, perform welding tasks, and operate paint sprayers. They can also perform delicate tasks like embedding computer chips in dashboards.

Rethink Robotics in Boston built a robot named Sawyer to fabricate metal, assemble circuit boards, and load and unload parts. Rethink Robotics vice president Matt Fitzgerald describes Sawyer as a big bundle of sensors: "Sawyer has an embedded camera in the robot for locating parts before picking or placing. You can track . . . how much force was used when placing something into a fixture. It can tell you the run-time hours and the parts count."[9]

Artificial Intelligence

Industrial robots are evolving rapidly as computer engineers develop next-gen machines that are autonomous. These robots run on artificial intelligence (AI), computer "brains" that can reason and learn. AI computers rely on automatic code generation; the machines can adjust, produce, or change their programming depending on the situation. A good example of this machine learning can be seen in the Tesla Model S electric car, which can drive semi-autonomously. The autopilot feature on the Tesla allows the car to collect millions of miles of driving data from its human drivers. Sensors pick up information about acceleration, braking, and even driver hand placement on the steering wheel and other controls. Instead of programming the car to drive autonomously, the car learns on its own by observing human drivers. As Tesla chief executive officer (CEO) and computer engineer Elon Musk explains, each driver becomes "an expert trainer."[10] The cars also communicate with one another over the Tesla network to share the driving knowledge they pick up from their expert trainers. The information is used to create what are called data maps that contain the average speed, traffic patterns, and hazards found on specific stretches of highway. This information is transmitted to any Tesla that travels on the road and helps the car better navigate stop-and-go traffic, rain, snow, and other conditions.

"Many [artificial intelligence] accomplishments were made possible because of advances in hardware. Hardware is the foundation of everything you can do."[12]

—MIT engineering professor Joel Emer

In 2018 the field of artificial intelligence was still in its infancy. As language expert Erik Cambria notes, "There is [no machine] today that is even barely as intelligent as the most stupid human being on Earth."[11] But the field is rapidly advancing, and computer engineers are designing the instruments necessary to create the AI systems of the future. As MIT professor Joel Emer points out: "The value of the hardware at the heart of [AI] is often overlooked. . . . Many AI accomplishments were made possible because of advances in hardware. Hardware is the foundation of everything you can do in software."[12]

Quantum Computing

Perhaps the most advanced work performed by computer engineers is taking place in the field of quantum computing. Quantum computers function much differently than digital computers. Conventional computers process data encoded in binary digits, or bits. Each bit can only be defined as one or zero. Quantum computers work with quantum bits, or qubits, that exist on an atomic level. Qubits can exist in multiple states, which allow them to transmit information many times faster than binary digital computers. As might be expected, the science behind quantum computing is extremely complex. Single phosphorus atoms embedded in silicon can become entangled with one another to produce what are called logical qubits. These particles can theoretically communicate with one another. A computer using just three hundred logical qubits would possess more computing power than all the world's conventional computers connected together.

The field of medicine is expected to provide one of the main applications for quantum computers. Qubits could be used to rapidly sequence a patient's genes in seconds and evaluate all the possible interactions between molecules, proteins, and chemicals. This would allow for personalized drug treatment.

The Brain-Computer Interface

Quantum computing is at the heart of Musk's 2017 venture called Neuralink. The company is working to develop what Musk calls a brain-computer interface. Such devices could theoretically be implanted in the brain to help humans merge with computer software programs. Musk believes that humans will need a brain-computer interface in the future to communicate directly with machines while keeping pace with artificial intelligence.

Musk notes that some computers communicate at a rate of a trillion bits per second, while a human typing on a smartphone is limited to ten bits per second. He believes that tiny, implantable computers need to be created so that humans and machines can achieve some sort of balance. As Musk told an audience at the World Government Summit in Dubai in 2017: "Over time I think we will probably see a closer merger of biological intelligence and digital intelligence. It's mostly about the bandwidth, the speed of the connection between your brain and the digital version of yourself."[13]

Computer engineers will continue to be at the forefront of those who design and build the fastest, smartest, and smallest machines ever created. And today's computer engineering miracles will be overshadowed by the cutting-edge inventions of tomorrow. From satellites circling the earth to the atomic particles surging through the brain, computer engineers are the pioneers leading a digital revolution that continues to transform society and culture in ways simple and profound.

CHAPTER 2

How Do You Become a Computer Engineer?

A bachelor of science degree in computer engineering or a related subject is required by all employers that produce computer hardware. And students wishing to become computer engineers need to become proficient in many complex subjects. While this might feel overwhelming, prospective computer engineers can get a head start on their careers by making high school count.

Many of the courses needed for a computer science degree can be first taken in high school. For example, math is the foundation for all computer science, and students should take as many math courses as possible. As Google software engineer Eric Willisson explains, "Math classes are good because they help you learn to think in the logical ways that help with computers. Algebra is useful for understanding many algorithms later, geometry helps if you're going to do any graphics and can help with graph theory (which, again, helps with many algorithms), and I have always found calculus showing up in unexpected places."[14]

> "Math classes are good because they help you learn to think in the logical ways that help with computers."[14]
>
> —Eric Willisson, software engineer

Any technology using electricity, mechanics, heat, light, sound, and optics is based on physics. Since computers use all of the above, prospective computer engineers should add physics classes to their high school curriculum. The courses teach about how things work while breaking them down into smaller and smaller components to see how each bit functions independently. Computer engineering is almost entirely applied physics, and the study of physics will help prospective computer engineers grasp how circuits, processors, and other components function.

Tech Camps

Prospective computer engineering students can get a jump-start on college by attending tech summer camps. These camps, designed for future computer engineers, coders, and other tech lovers, provide a great way for students to learn while they have fun. Weeklong summer iD Tech Camps are offered at more than eighty prestigious universities in thirty states from coast to coast. Summer iD Tech Camps are also available to students in Hong Kong, Singapore, and the United Kingdom. Cutting-edge programs are tailored to various age groups from seven through seventeen. High school students can learn to code apps and games, create and code wearable tech, build robots, and study artificial intelligence and machine learning.

The Digital Media Academy is another summer camp that spotlights STEM (science, technology, engineering, and math) subjects. The academy was founded in 2002, and since that time over 155,000 students have learned and lived at college campuses in the United States and Canada, including Northwestern, Duke, University of Washington, and University of Toronto. Campers study programming, robotics, engineering, and other topics of interest to future computer engineers.

Beyond science, prospective computer engineers need to be able to write well and communicate clearly. High school students should not neglect English classes, as Willisson explains: "Programmers who document their code well are few, far between, and highly valuable."[15] In addition many computer professionals found that classes in art, philosophy, history, and music helped them solve problems by thinking more creatively. According to an unnamed source quoted in the *Princeton Review*: "One of the biggest surprises in my 25 years of technology work is that people who have a creative background . . . [tend to] see and grasp big-picture concepts very quickly, and break them down into subcomponents. People who [only] have a computer engineering or math background tend to be very technical, and sometimes that can be a hindrance."[16]

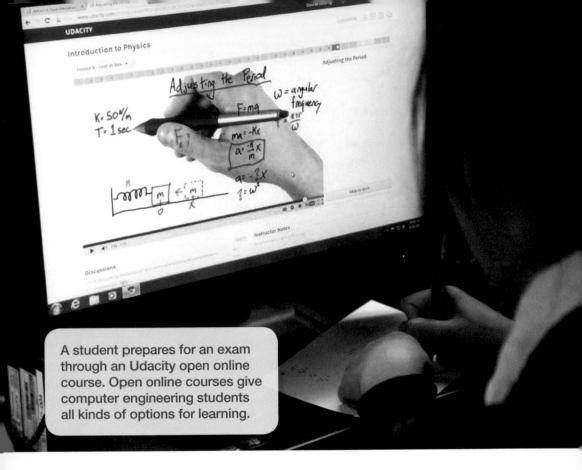

A student prepares for an exam through an Udacity open online course. Open online courses give computer engineering students all kinds of options for learning.

Massive Open Online Courses

Every computer engineer needs strong programming skills so that writing code becomes second nature. High school students should be familiar with programming languages such as AngularJS, Python, JavaScript, Ruby, and C++. High school students, college students, and anyone else who wants to learn to code or improve their programming skills can visit the website Codecademy. The site is categorized as a Massive Open Online Course, or MOOC. These open online courses offer access to classes on the web with unlimited participation. Codecademy provides free interactive coding classes in twelve different programming languages. For around twenty dollars a month, coders can sign up for "Pro" classes, which offer more personalized training.

The web offers numerous other free or inexpensive MOOCs that can help prepare high school students for a career in computer engineering. Over 29 million people have registered to take classes at Coursera, which hosts over two thousand courses from top-rated colleges and universities, including Stanford, Yale, and Princeton. The site features courses in algorithms, artificial intelligence, programming languages, machine learning, and other subjects of interest for future computer engineers. Some of the online courses might be too advanced for the average high school student. However, the classes can shine a light on the world of computer engineering while providing inexpensive guidance. As computer engineering and Coursera student Feynman Liang explains, "I get to gain a nontrivial understanding of a field. And it translates into me doing a lot better in college. . . . You really don't need a certificate or official recognition for what you take away from the classes [for them] to be useful to you."[17]

Several other popular MOOCs offer classes aimed at prospective computer engineers. The edX website, which provides free courses from Harvard, MIT, and nearly one hundred other institutions, emphasizes computer science, programming, and computer engineering. Udacity, which is sponsored by Amazon, Google, IBM, and other tech companies, offers courses in virtual reality development, engineering self-driving cars, and robotic engineering.

Precollege Summer School

High school students who prefer classroom learning over online courses can prep for a bachelor of science degree by attending summer school at colleges and universities. Summer school, referred to as precollege summer programs, offers high school students opportunities to expand their knowledge. Participants might also make valuable connections with professors who can write letters of recommendation to include with college applications.

While hundreds of colleges offer summer precollege programs, the University of California (UC) system is ranked among the best. Open to students in grades nine through twelve, the UC Summer School for Mathematics and Science is a four-week residential program. Topics extend beyond typical curricula found in high schools, with a strong emphasis on science, technology, and computer engineering. Several courses are of interest to prospective computer engineers. Robot Inventors offers students the opportunity to build their own robots. Another course called Engineering Design and Control of Kinetic Sculptures focuses on utilizing microprocessors, microcontrollers, and other hardware to build sculptures that climb, bounce, fall, and perform other movements.

Stanford University is working to increase diversity in the computer engineering field with its Artificial Intelligence Laboratory's Outreach Summer Program. The course is open to girls who are interested in exploring hardware and software used for AI applications. The two-week class provides faculty lectures, field trips, hands-on projects, and mentoring sessions.

Cornell University in Ithaca, New York, is a top-rated engineering school and offers the Cornell Engineering Experience, a six-week residential summer program. The courses focus on math, computer science, and physics. Precollege students combine lab work with cutting-edge research and are able to meet with the college's engineering professors and representatives from its admissions office.

Other top-rated precollege programs include Harvard University's Secondary School Program, Johns Hopkins University's Engineering Innovation, and the Computational Science Class for High School Students at Illinois Tech in Chicago. The Game Lab Summer Institute at University of California, Los Angeles (UCLA) is perhaps the most unique precollege summer technology program. The two-week course offers instruction in video and mobile games and gaming hardware.

Obtain a Bachelor's Degree

Completion of a precollege summer program provides a great addition to a college application, but it is not mandatory. High school students wishing to enroll in a computer engineering degree program should choose a school that is certified by the Accreditation Board for Engineering and Technology (ABET). This organization provides assurance that programs meet the quality standards of the engineering profession. In 2018 ABET accredited over 3,800 programs at 770 colleges and universities in thirty-one countries.

Coursework for a four-year bachelor's degree in computer engineering covers subjects specific to the field. Core computer engineering classes include introduction to software engineering, computer programming, computer architecture, applied algorithms for engineering, microprocessors, electrical design, signal processing, logic design, and mathematical structures related to computer hardware and software. Other coursework covers scientific subjects such as physics and chemistry.

While the coursework may sound dizzying, the lab work can be fun, according to Nishil Shah, a computer engineering student at the University of Texas:

> I got to take an advanced embedded systems lab course where my group chose to build a Bluetooth music player as our final project. We did all of the circuit and [circuit board] work like integrating the speakers, the processor, resistors, the Bluetooth module, an SD card, the LCD screen, and much more. We also wrote the software so you could select which song to play and how to store a song on the SD card that was being downloaded via Bluetooth.[18]

Benefits of a Graduate Degree

Many good jobs are available for those with bachelor's degrees in computer engineering. But according to a 2017 study by the job information organization CareerOneStop, 26 percent of computer engineers hold a master's degree. These professionals obtain the best positions and highest salaries, and they oversee the most interesting projects.

Students pursuing a master of science in computer engineering spend their first year completing course requirements that emphasize cybersecurity, computer connections and networks, and computer hardware architecture. Second-year students pursue specific areas of interest, often in computer science or electrical engineering. Other classes include systems engineering, computer systems security foundations, probability for computer and electrical engineers, broadband network architectures, and modern active circuit design. Most master's programs incorporate what are called capstone projects in the final year. A capstone

Work as an Intern

Whatever a computer engineer's educational background might be, an internship will provide some of the vital experience that managers look for on a résumé. Internships provide hands-on development experience and knowledge of hardware and software systems. Those who work as interns often find mentors who help them learn. Florida International University computer engineering student Alastair Paragas describes the benefits of his internship at CERN, home of the hadron collider in Geneva, Switzerland: "[I was able to] network with highly intelligent people coming from diverse fields of study, ranging from physics, mathematics, mechanical engineering and computer science. I am always humbled working with behemoths from their respective fields, living and working on the shoulders of giants."

Professors often link students to internships, but positions can be obtained by e-mailing the numerous tech companies that offer summer intern positions. Candidates work with teams in a fast-moving environment to integrate, deploy, and support complex computer systems. Interns participate in research and development, problem-solving, maintenance, and other tasks. To qualify for internships, candidates are required to be enrolled in a college or university, and they must be familiar with various computer hardware, operating systems, and coding.

Quoted in Millie Acebal, "My Internship with CERN," FIU News, May 15, 2017. https://news.fiu.edu.

project is a question or problem that students choose and pursue independent research on the subject.

Those who wish to teach at the university level or conduct computer engineering research need to obtain a doctorate (PhD), which requires a four- to seven-year commitment. This process requires students to be accepted into a program, complete course work, and write a lengthy research-based essay called a dissertation. Pinterest product engineer Tracy Chou describes how participating in a PhD program helped her personal growth:

You pick up research and critical thinking skills. You learn to think independently. . . . You learn how to break down problems, and set about seeking to solve them. You learn to be self-motivated, because a PhD program is so free-form that you'll have to set your own schedule and deadlines. You get to spend a few years thinking deeply about a problem that you're interested in . . . without the pressure of a boss who needs something for a product deadline or a company that needs to hit revenue targets or other such external constraints.[19]

Chou lists disadvantages as well. Holders of PhDs are over-qualified for many computer industry jobs, which means they might only be able to initially find work as coders. This would make it difficult to defray the added costs of obtaining a doctorate degree. Additionally, employers often view doctoral candidates, who spent years in academic settings, as out of touch with the latest advances in industry. And most start-ups cannot afford to hire PhDs. But, according to Chou, the advantages of obtaining a PhD outweigh the disadvantages: "Some of the more prestigious director or VP roles are reserved for people who have PhDs, especially if they are to oversee very technical areas. [And] if you get very, very lucky, you can start a company to commercialize your research in a field with a high barrier to entry because of the technical depth."[20]

Get Certified

Certification is not required for a career in computer engineering. However, certification serves as a badge of approval, and those who hold official credentials can expect higher wages. The Institute of Electrical and Electronics Engineers (IEEE) is the primary organization that provides software certification for computer engineers. The IEEE awards various certifications to those who complete an extensive two-part online exam. A passing score qualifies an individual as a Certified Software Development Professional (CSDP).

Other certifications are awarded by vendors to those who specialize in their systems. Cisco, which builds networking hardware and other high-tech equipment, offers a certification ladder. It starts on lower rungs and moves up to more complex certifications. For example, the Cisco Certified Design Associate (CCDA) and Cisco Certified Design Professional (CCDP) certifications can lead to jobs in computer networking architecture. Computer engineers can continue to climb up the certification ladder by obtaining the Cisco Certified Design Expert (CCDE), which is a prerequisite for the Cisco Certified Architect (CCAr). At this level a computer engineer can also obtain certifications in Cisco Certified Internetwork Expert (CCIE), Routing and Switching or Data Center.

"You will have to constantly learn. You need to be very much aware of not just the technologies available today but about the trends."[21]

—Peter Steenkiste, professor of computer engineering

Obtaining certification is part of the lifelong learning process associated with the computer engineering profession. Computer engineers constantly update their knowledge. They read books and journals, attend conferences, and take classes to stay informed about the latest changes in technology. As professor of computer engineering at Carnegie Mellon University Peter Steenkiste explains, "You will have to constantly learn. You need to be very much aware of not just the technologies available today but about the trends."[21]

It takes great dedication to earn a degree in computer engineering, but it is not all hard work. And many students who major in computer engineering say they love the hands-on projects, the teamwork, the design competitions, and other features of the program. The classes can make science and math lively and interesting, and a degree in computer engineering is a ticket to an exciting career marked by good pay, fascinating work, and next-gen research.

CHAPTER 3

What Skills and Personal Qualities Matter Most— and Why?

Engineers are highly respected professionals, but they often battle common misconceptions about their vocation. Engineers are often painted as introverted, math-loving nerds who lack creative skills. Mechanical engineer Brandon R. Buckhalt founded the Creative Engineer website to dispel the stereotypes: "Engineers are the builders, the believers, the inventors, the creative geniuses, and the optimistic go-getters that have guided our civilization out of the caves and onto the moon."[22]

The term *engineer* comes from the Latin word for ingenuity, *ingeniator*. And engineers have historically been viewed as inventive people, those who use ingenuity and creative thought processes to solve problems. At the same time, engineering requires a great deal of personal discipline since the highly technical work can be brutally difficult. Buckhalt's wife, Lisa, is also an engineer, and she offers her summation of the work: "Engineering requires the fortitude to enthusiastically apply your energy toward a task you find undesirable."[20]

> "Engineers are the builders, the believers, the inventors, the creative geniuses, and the optimistic go-getters that have guided our civilization out of the caves and onto the moon."[22]
>
> —Brandon R. Buckhalt, mechanical engineer

Enthusiastically applying energy to difficult tasks requires skills that fit into three broad categories. Computer engineers rely on technical skills, operational skills, and what might be called character skills. Education forms the basis for technical skills that

Computer engineers typically work in teams. This requires solid communication skills as well as the ability to cooperate with colleagues who might be working hundreds or thousands of miles away.

computer engineers use to analyze and understand problems. Internships and job experience provide operational skills that computer engineers rely on to perform experiments and complete tasks. Character skills are those that help computer engineers work well with others. They include self-motivation, determination, passion for the work, good communication abilities, and the capacity to work seamlessly as a team player.

Technical Skills

Technical skills are also called *hard skills*, a term that can have two meanings. Hard skills provide a rock-solid basis of knowledge required for computer engineering. Hard skills are also hard to master. That is why some students of computer architecture refer to the classes as "computer archi-torture." Joking aside, the job of a computer engineer is to utilize hard skills like science, technology, engineering, and math to design systems, run tests, and invent solutions to problems. Technical knowledge includes a good understanding of circuit boards, processors, chips, computer hardware and software, networking equipment, and other electronics.

While computer engineers are not necessarily "mathletes," they do rely on a strong understanding of mathematics to invent systems, components, and processes. Computer engineers use differential equations and linear algebra when working with circuits. And they use math skills to create algorithms. As computer engineer Naman Attri writes, "If you know how to build algorithms, learning any programming language becomes a piece of cake."[24]

While computer programs can be used to solve mathematical problems, computer engineers still need razor-sharp math skills. As engineering career counselor Alison Doyle explains, "The existence of computers does not free you from the need to understand math. In fact, since computers can only follow instructions, engineers must first figure out how to solve numeric problems on their own before they can tell a computer what to do."[25]

While computer engineers create their own programs and apps, they also work with computer modeling software, which is used to create complex systems and conduct experiments to ensure the systems work. Computer modeling methodology is used to design components and observe them from different points of view. Computer engineers also rely on modeling programs to produce techniques for building hardware.

Computer engineers draw on their analytical skills to identify the strengths and weaknesses of experiments. They use impartial analysis to evaluate the technical solutions that result from the experimentation. A talent for logic and reasoning helps computer engineers find solutions that function within the framework of budgets, production schedules, and other business concerns.

Operational Skills

As the name implies, operational skills help computer engineers operate efficiently on a day-to-day basis. Attention to detail is an operational skill especially important in the computer engineering field. Computer engineers work with intricate parts, such as circuits and processors, and search for the tiniest bugs and glitches in computer programs. These professionals must not only have an eye for detail when examining physical structures or lines of code, but they also need to be patient and persistent when solving problems.

Problem-solving and critical-thinking skills work together to help a computer engineer identify a problem and evaluate solutions to find the proper remedy. Multitasking skills are important for computer engineers who need to remain organized and focused while simultaneously dealing with puzzling plans, tiny pieces of hardware, and demands from production managers and CEOs.

Computer engineers need to be good readers who can learn from manuals, technical journals, and periodicals. Reading helps engineers identify new design tools, implement recent technology, and keep up with changes in the industry. Computer engineers also need to be adept at technical writing to describe complex concepts in a clear, concise manner. Computer engineers are often called upon to write memos and instruct less technically inclined employees on numerous issues from implementing new algorithms to using recently developed equipment.

> "I have met very few engineers who are comfortable with using simple language, organizing documents for the readers' benefit, keeping sentences and paragraphs short, and getting to the point."[26]
>
> —Gary Blake, technical writing instructor

Computer engineers also write scientific papers for technical periodicals and for presentations at conferences. Beyond technical subjects, most computer engineers are expected to write trip reports, business proposals, and reports on lab experiments. This operational skill, while particularly important, is a rarity in the computer engineering field, as technical writing instructor Gary Blake points out: "In my 25 years of teaching seminars in technical writing, I have met very few engineers who are comfortable with using simple language, organizing documents for the readers' benefit, keeping sentences and paragraphs short, and getting to the point."[26]

This advice carries over to conversation. Computer engineers sometimes need to be reminded to speak in sentences rather than long-winded paragraphs. They need to translate the technical language of computer engineering into plain English for multiple stakeholders in a project, which might include bosses, assistants, marketing executives, and customers. As executive coach Stacey Hanke explains, people are bombarded with messages all day: "Speaking in short bullet point sentences, pausing to allow your listeners to stay with you will help you be heard above the noise."[27]

Character Skills

Character skills are sometimes referred to as soft skills, which generally refer to the capacity to work well with others. An engineering blogger known as 3DX explains: "Nobody completes an engineering project by themselves: there is a vast team working on various parts of the project."[28] This means computer engineers must work well with groups that might include members from culturally diverse research teams, global corporations, and experts from other scientific disciplines. Workplace expert Amy Cooper Hakim explains that character skills cannot be learned in a classroom: "[A computer engineer] can be taught how to use a certain computer program much more quickly than she can be taught how to establish rapport or trust with a colleague or customer. Bosses look for those with excellent [character] skills to lead others, to gain customers and to share and promote ideas in group settings."[29]

While character skills come naturally to some, others need to make an effort to perfect them. Job counselors say interactions with others are made easier by making eye contact. Looking into a person's eyes helps establish trust, and as economist Joseph Stiglitz wrote in 2013, "It's trust, more than money, that makes the world go round."[30] This is especially true for computer engineers who are seeking employment. According to a poll by the job recruiting website iCims, 68 percent of job recruiters say the most common mistake job applicants make is avoiding eye contact.

Establishing trust is also important for computer engineers who work as team leaders. Coworkers listen better when trust is established, and they will take risks if they know they will be supported if projects do not go as planned. Team leaders also rely on character skills to motivate others. They provide clear guidance

Hard Skills and Soft Skills

In past decades employers were mostly interested in job applicants who possessed hard skills, the technical engineering abilities necessary to perform specific tasks. However, in recent years job recruiters are placing much more importance on soft skills that include communication, professionalism, and enthusiasm. Career expert Alison Doyle delves into the differences between hard and soft skills:

> Hard skills are teachable abilities or skill sets that are easy to quantify. Typically, you'll learn hard skills in the classroom, through books or other training materials, or on the job. . . . Soft skills, on the other hand, are subjective skills that are much harder to quantify. Also known as "people skills" or "interpersonal skills," soft skills relate to the way you relate to and interact with other people. Examples of soft skills include communication, flexibility, leadership, motivation, patience . . . problem solving abilities, teamwork, time management, [and] work ethic.
>
> While certain hard skills are necessary for any position, employers increasingly look for job applicants with particular soft skills. This is because, while it is easy for an employer to train a new employee in a particular hard skill (such as how to use a certain computer program), it is much more difficult to train an employee in a soft skill (such as patience).

Alison Doyle, "Hard Skills vs. Soft Skills: What's the Difference?," Balance Careers, March 21, 2018. www.thebalance.com.

and direction and willingly listen to others. They know when to step in to help struggling coworkers and when to back off.

Leaders need to understand how to utilize the strengths of others while setting realistic goals. They do not create schedules or develop plans that are too ambitious. Additionally, leaders must have high ethical standards and a strong sense of professionalism.

Time at Work

While the people they work with and the challenges they encounter often change daily, the majority of mechanical engineers work full time, forty hours a week. Overtime can be a regular part of the job, though. According to the Bureau of Labor Statistics (BLS), 30 percent of mechanical engineers worked more than forty hours per week in 2016. In general, mechanical engineers are salaried employees.

Often, the amount of time a mechanical engineer works depends on the company and what is currently happening with projects. The culture of a company may be one in which it is expected that engineers work sixty-plus hours a week, but others may promote a more equal work-family balance. As for projects, at times they require travel or extra hours if at a critical juncture. For Brianne Hamilton, her typical workweek is more than forty hours but less than fifty, which is a good balance in her mind.

> "My role as a Product Engineer has me working with various departments, including customer service, operations, supply, quality and aftermarket."[19]
>
> —Seng Chang, product mechanical engineer

I feel like when I go home I can focus on other things, and I don't take my work home with me often (though I do think about it and sometimes have dreams where I'm trying to figure out a problem). There was a time a couple of years ago where I was travelling about once a month, working on a manufacturing line and doing some testing with doctors out of state. However, in general, I feel like the work-life balance is great.[20]

Compensation

Because the job of a mechanical engineer is challenging and requires a higher-level education, the compensation is fairly high in comparison with other careers. According to the BLS, the median salary of a mechanical engineer was $84,190, equivalent to

$40.48 an hour, in 2016. Compared to the median pay of all workers, $37,040, a mechanical engineer makes a lucrative salary.

A mechanical engineer's pay scale depends on many variables, including location, industry, job responsibility, years at the company, and experience. According to *U.S. News & World Report*, industry and employer have a major effect on a mechanical engineer's salary. The places of employment with the highest average annual salaries are oil and gas extraction ($131,900), software publishers ($120,650), electronic and precision equipment repair and maintenance ($116,440), waste treatment and disposal ($112,310), and pipeline transportation of crude oil ($111,600). Additionally, the highest-paid work is in the metropolitan areas of Anchorage, Alaska; Tuscaloosa, Alabama; and Taunton, Massachusetts. In Anchorage the average salary of a mechanical engineer is $145,900.

> "The cool thing about a job in mechanical engineering is that there is no typical day."[21]
>
> —Yassmin Abdel-Magied, mechanical engineer

Job Satisfaction

Overall, mechanical engineers are satisfied with their careers, according to *U.S. News & World Report*. In general, they feel encouraged by opportunities for upward mobility. They also say they experience moderate levels of stress and enjoy above-average flexibility in connection with their work schedules. According to the Institution of Mechanical Engineers, 89 percent of engineers have high levels of job satisfaction and would choose the same career again.

Many mechanical engineers attribute the overall job satisfaction to the variety the career affords. Yassmin Abdel-Magied, a well engineer with the Shell Oil Company, considers this fact the best part about the job. Abdel-Magied explains:

> The cool thing about a job in mechanical engineering is that there is no typical day. Generally, my current role has two sides to it; onshore and offshore. When I'm onshore, I spend my time helping to prepare for drilling projects,

working with geologists to understand what's under ground and then figure out the best rig for each hole. When I'm offshore working on a rig, I'm supporting the Drilling Supervisor, organizing people to get the job done right and designing solutions to make things happen. It's hard work but definitely fun and exciting to see our plans turn into reality.[21]

Overall, mechanical engineers like Abdel-Magied are satisfied with their careers. The pay, work-life balance, and changing nature of their work keeps them content. The possibility of future advancement adds to the excitement of future opportunities in their careers.

CHAPTER 5

Advancement and Other Job Opportunities

Most mechanical engineers begin with an entry-level position in whatever industry they enter. Typical titles of entry-level mechanical engineering positions include assistant mechanical engineer, team member, associate engineer, and mechanical engineer I. Usually, an engineer in one of these jobs will be assigned to a team, group, or specific project with other more senior engineers and will be supervised by a manager.

At larger companies, entry-level mechanical engineers are often specialized and are assigned to work on a specific critical component of a larger machine, system, or product. For example, a mechanical engineer at an automotive company might work solely on a brake pad of a vehicle to ensure it meets the specifications of the designers. In comparison, at a smaller company, an entry-level engineer might work with everyone on a team to create an entirely new device.

The type of work entry-level engineers do is based on their specific job but is likely to include basics of design, testing, or analysis. Specific types of daily tasks may include researching problems to solve, sketching out potential design solutions, constructing prototypes, testing prototypes to see if they meet specifications, obtaining feedback on products from customers and sharing it with the team, and observing processes of production to analyze what might produce better outputs.

Technical Advancement

After working as an entry-level mechanical engineer for some time, many apply for advancement either within their company

Mechanical engineers who want to advance their careers often become team leaders. They help coordinate large projects and work closely with team members to meet a client's needs and timeline.

or by moving to another company. Advancing as a mechanical engineer usually involves either following a technical or managerial track. Those who follow a technical track tend to be more hands-on and are involved in prototypes and testing of their designs. Types of technical advancement jobs are technical lead, head engineer, and senior engineer. Those in these positions remain heavily involved in the actual mechanical engineering aspect of the job, while some may also incorporate management and leadership skills to guide a project or team.

Dan Foran was a senior mechanical engineer at iRobot, where he worked on a specific home care product. His job was to lead a team of engineers who designed products for delivery to a production facility in Asia, where hundreds of thousands of robots per year are made and shipped all over the world. An additional duty of his job was to help run the company's internship program, working with the company's interns to train them to work as full-time engineers.

Many on the technical track seek out more certification and education to make them eligible for more promotional opportunities. These include obtaining a PE license and/or a master of science in mechanical or other type of engineering. The PE license allows a person to legally sign off on designs. It is not just higher degrees that are required for promotions, however. A demonstrated ability to work well with others and the ability to communicate and understand the big picture are also a necessity. A mechanical engineer who is able to show that he or she is highly skilled at his or her job, understands a specific area well, and is looked to by others for technical support will be able to advance in the field. "For example, if you have strong analytical skills, you might become a company expert with finite element analysis software," writes Auston Matta, an engineer in the packaging industry. "These software programs allow engineers to refine and validate designs early in the engineering process without the added expense of physical testing. Building experience in this area would be beneficial and could lead to a senior-level promotion."[22]

Combining Business and Engineering

Mechanical engineers may also seek out a managerial track. Their technical ability will allow them to understand the products of the company, how the equipment works to produce the products, and all of the processes to develop the products or systems. They then combine this with communication, accounting, marketing, and other business skills that allow them to run different aspects of a program or project.

Those who choose this route may advance to a supervisor, manager, plant manager, or executive within a company. They usually pursue further classes in accounting, marketing, organizational flow, and supply management. Some obtain a master's degree in business administration or other management-related degrees to become more eligible for jobs in management. Matta obtained his master's degree in engineering management and rose to management-level engineering positions within the packaging industry. Matta explains the types of responsibilities a project engineer would typically have in a company:

You will have a budget and will decide how and when to spend the company's money. You will spend a lot of time working with colleagues in other departments. Your daily tasks will shift from technical to decision-making and project management, so your days of CAD work or running tests in the mechanical analysis lab will be over. Instead, you'll be in charge of scheduling testing and prioritizing projects for your engineering team.[23]

For Heather Clarke, combining the skills of engineering and business is essential to success at her job. Clarke is a business

Rising Through the Ranks

The US Navy needs engineers in order to keep its ships, submarines, aircraft, and bases running. Engineers are typically officers and are able to advance through the ranks, eventually running departments as higher-level officers if they qualify. Captain Mark Oesterreich graduated from the US Naval Academy with a degree in naval architecture, and a few years after becoming an officer, he received his master of science in mechanical engineering and a PE license at the Naval Postgraduate School. Oesterreich has served for over twenty years at various naval commands in engineering positions of increasing responsibility. Today Oesterreich is the commanding officer at Naval Surface Warfare Center, Crane Division. Over the years, as he served on ships and submarines, Oesterreich learned how to deal with maintenance of systems in all types of situations, a lesson that helped his success at each duty station. "If something breaks, you've got to fix it. If there's a critical attribute to a particular maintenance item or a particular operation, you have to make sure the right people are there to verify that critical attribute is met," Oesterreich says.

Quoted in NSCW Crane Public Affairs, "Meet NSWC Crane's New Commanding Officer: Capt. Mark Oesterreich," Naval Sea Systems Command, July 24, 2017. www.navsea.navy.mil.

operations manager at Atkins Global, a design, engineering, and project management consultancy, and is in charge of a team of fifty health, safety, and environmental engineers in the oil and gas sector. She is responsible for the day-to-day care of the team, the profit-and-loss accounts, and future project planning and growth. She spends much of her time with her staff, helping them with the logistics of projects. Additionally, Clarke says, "I review project proposals before they are submitted to the client to ensure that the methodology and pricing is in line with expectations. The rest of my time is generally spent answering emails and questions relating to the running of the business group and strategy for the future."[24] Clarke estimates that 80 percent of her daily routine involves communication, both within her team and with others inside her organization.

Academic Opportunities

Another option is academia. This attracts mechanical engineers interested in designing and making prototypes of the latest technology. In this field, advancement often takes the form of becoming an assistant or associate professor, following a tenure track to full professorship. To achieve this, mechanical engineers must obtain a PhD in engineering and complete a thesis on a topic related to their area of interest. They will then teach classes and conduct research projects.

Michele Miller is a mechanical engineering professor at Michigan Technological University. She received her bachelor of science from Duke University and her master of science and PhD in mechanical engineering from North Carolina State University. Initially, she worked in the automotive industry but realized she wanted to be more hands-on with research and switched to a career in academics. Miller says:

"I spend a lot of time reading about the latest technology developments, writing about my research, giving presentations about my research, preparing material for classes, teaching classes, and meeting with students."[25]

—Michele Miller, mechanical engineering professor

Intern to CEO

Ursula Burns, the former CEO and chair of Xerox Corporation, grew up in a poor neighborhood with a mother who advocated for her education. She ended up in mechanical engineering because she liked math and someone suggested engineering. Burns then earned a bachelor of science in mechanical engineering from the Polytechnic Institute of NYU and a master of science in mechanical engineering from Columbia University. "My entire existence, my business personality, my practices at work—how I lead, manage, and interact—the foundation of it all is my engineering education," says Burns. "I moved from engineering to business but the difference is not a difference at all. The synergy between the two is amazing." She joined Xerox in 1980 as a mechanical engineering summer intern and then was promoted throughout her career until 2009, when she became the company's CEO and made history as the first African American woman to lead a Fortune 500 company. Today, she is the chairwoman of the board for Veon, a multinational telecommunications company.

Quoted in Chitra Sethi, "Ursula Burns: From Engineer to CEO," American Society of Mechanical Engineers, 2015. www.asme.org.

Working at a university as a graduate student and now as a professor has allowed me to do more hands-on work and spend less time doing paperwork or making phone calls. My job as a professor has a lot of variety. In addition to the laboratory activities, I spend a lot of time reading about the latest technology developments, writing about my research, giving presentations about my research, preparing material for classes, teaching classes, and meeting with students.[25]

Miller specifically works with graduate students on research projects involving the development of microelectromechanical systems, in which they conduct laboratory experiments and computer analysis as part of their research.

Owning a Business

Some mechanical engineers realize that they are interested in running their own company or consultancy. They may create a company that designs and creates prototypes and machines or provides other mechanical engineer services. In addition to mechanical engineering skills, those who choose this route need to understand business essentials, such as marketing and accounting, and how to organize and oversee employees if they hire others.

Subi Shah decided he wanted to be his own boss rather than work for a company, and after years in the industry, he left to become a mechanical design consultant. As a consultant he decides which clients to work for and which projects to do and is flexible with his time. He is also under constant pressure to find new clients and jobs. Shah takes his clients' ideas and turns them into physical components, such as an insert for a blender or a mountable light fixture. He additionally designs, models, and develops prototypes of new products. Sometimes he hires subcontractors if the project involves electrical work. Shah has discovered that his own consultancy requires a lot of coordination, planning, and budgeting to keep it successful. "Freelancing can be great, but it's definitely not the same as having a salaried job," writes Shah. "Sometimes you'll have a lot of work, sometimes none. It's just like riding a bike: It's really hard at first, and then you have to constantly pay attention to your surroundings to succeed."[26]

> "It's just like riding a bike: It's really hard at first, and then you have to constantly pay attention to your surroundings to succeed."[26]
>
> —Subi Shah, mechanical engineer freelance consultant

Mechanical engineers often find that roads to advancement can vary. Whether as the chief executive officer (CEO) of a machine tooling company or the owner of a design consultancy, the possibility to achieve career success is there.

CHAPTER 6

What Does the Future Hold for Mechanical Engineers?

Graduating with a degree in mechanical engineering assures a high possibility of obtaining a job with growth potential. Mechanical engineering jobs are growing each year. According to the BLS, the field is expected to grow 9 percent between 2016 and 2026, which equates to 25,300 new positions in the United States. This is due to the fact that as industries such as automotive and manufacturing grow, they will require more mechanical engineers.

Going Green

Mechanical engineers are needed in new and growing industries because of their ability to understand mechanical systems, thermodynamics, materials, and power. For example, as concern about the environment grows, more companies want to ensure both their production processes and their products are sustainable and "clean."

David Dornfeld has a PhD in mechanical engineering and is a professor of manufacturing engineering at the University of California–Berkeley, in addition to serving as the director of the university's Laboratory for Manufacturing and Sustainability. He sees understanding sustainability as key for up-and-coming mechanical and manufacturing engineers. "The need for efficient and effective use of energy, water, materials and other resources in manufacturing—and the desire to ensure that production does not cause adverse social impacts—requires making manufacturing more sustainable,"[27] says Dornfeld. He writes a blog, *Green*

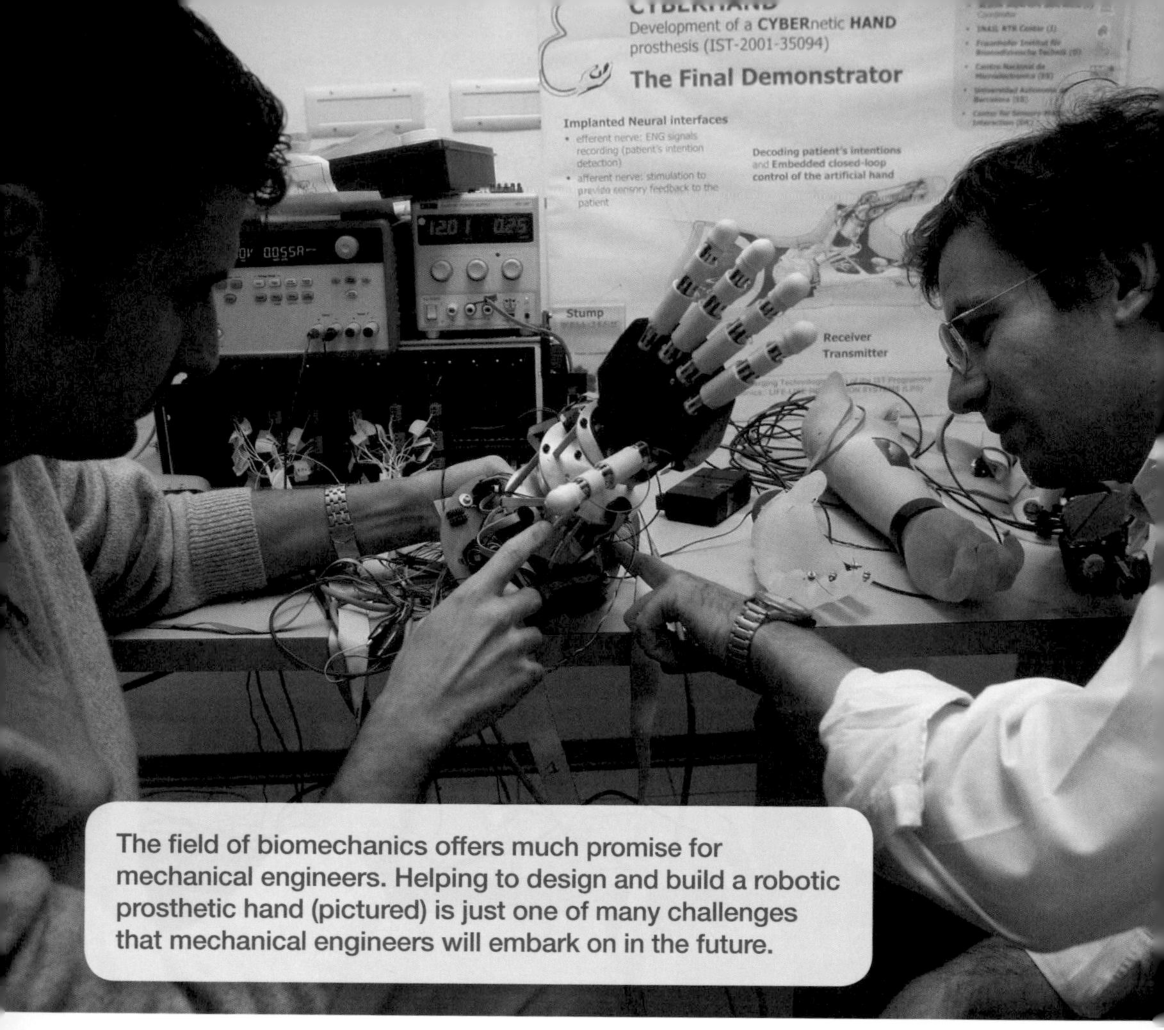

The field of biomechanics offers much promise for mechanical engineers. Helping to design and build a robotic prosthetic hand (pictured) is just one of many challenges that mechanical engineers will embark on in the future.

Manufacturing, that details the different ideas and ways he has learned and developed to integrate sustainability and environmentally friendly processes into mechanical and manufacturing development.

Examples of current mechanical engineering jobs specifically in the environmental area are green designers, who design, build, and maintain green buildings. These designs include energy sources, waste and water systems, and even landscaping. Another area is solar panel technology, which depends on different engineering disciplines, including mechanical, to create its products. This industry requires mechanical engineers, from design conception and prototype to installation and maintenance of solar panel technology. Solar technology is also enjoying rapid growth. According to the Solar Energy Industries Association, there were 1 million solar installations in the United States by 2016 and 2 million by 2018. The association projects 4 million solar installations by 2022.

The Latest Vehicles

The automotive industry is also rapidly responding to concerns about the environment. Automobiles are being designed to use green technologies and increase fuel economy. The field of hybrid and electric cars has presented mechanical engineers with a range of new opportunities in design, development, and production of these vehicles.

Lowering the cost of hybrid and electric cars is seen as a necessity to make them more accessible to people. Automotive professionals see the possibility of doing this through better manufacturing. "Manufacturing is always a challenge," writes Nicholas Roche, a mechanical engineer for Tesla, a leading maker of electric vehicles. "And as the [electric vehicle] industry scales up, there is going to be a lot of room for people who can figure out how to reduce the cost of manufacturing the batteries, motors, and power electronics that are at the heart of electric cars."[28]

Robotics Growth

Robotics, considered a branch of mechanical engineering, is seeing an increase in momentum as more companies are developing and using commercial robots in their processes. The BLS reports that from 2010 to 2017, US companies added 136,748 robots to factory floors. While robotic automation reduced the number of people required to perform robotic tasks, the number of skilled technicians needed to program, operate, and maintain those robots has increased. The BLS also reported that these robots created 894,000 new manufacturing jobs. Job growth in this field is likely to continue for the foreseeable future. In a 2015 National Robotics Education Foundation poll, two hundred senior corporate executives were asked about this. In that poll,

On Mars

Mechanical engineers are not confined to work on Earth. The National Aeronautics and Space Administration's (NASA) developments over the years have been the result of scores of engineers and scientists who have accomplished what many considered impossible. Megan Richardson, a mechanical engineer at NASA's Jet Propulsion Laboratory, is one of these. She "talks" to *Curiosity*, the rover that roams Mars, every day. She works on a team that builds a day's worth of commands for the rover to accomplish the following day and sends it to the rover. These commands may include driving to a new spot or brushing dust off a rock to secure a clear image of it to send back to Earth. Each day, the rover sends data to the lab, where Richardson and her team review the information to ensure the rover accomplished its assigned tasks and determine if changes are needed for the next set of instructions. Richardson has used her mechanical engineering background along with her ability to learn and analyze to become part of a mission beyond our planet.

81 percent of respondents agreed that robotics will experience significant job growth in the United States.

Beth Marcus, who holds a bachelor of science and master of science in mechanical engineering from MIT and a PhD in biomechanics from Imperial College London, is on the front line of robotics technology in manufacturing. She works as a senior principal technologist for Amazon Robotics and sees the result of her work at Amazon's fulfillment centers. Marcus says:

> We are on the precipice of huge advances in the field of robotics with the potential for new technology to become more deeply integrated into our every day lives. Contrary to what some may say, robotics simply make tasks more efficient and allows people to shift their focus to more sophisticated activities. It's exciting to see the pace of innovation and the potential that exists in robotics.[29]

Advancing Biomechanics

Biomechanics is another high-growth field for mechanical engineers, particularly those interested in the design aspect of mechanics and its integration with biology. A major area of biomechanics involves the design of prosthetics, mechanical devices that replace human limbs and artificial organs. In this area, mechanical engineers work with medical doctors to understand the needs of the human body and then use this information to develop these products.

In 2005 doctors amputated Craig Hutto's leg after a shark attacked him during a fishing trip off the coast of Florida. Two years later Hutto tested a new prosthetic leg being developed by mechanical engineer Michael Goldfarb and his team at Vanderbilt University. The prototype was light and delivered the torque and power Hutto needed to walk and even run. Since then, Goldfarb has developed a newer version that includes a computer, which allows for advanced range of motion in the joints. One motor controls the knee joint and another the ankle joint, with a computer board that tells the motors what to do with the joints. Work on prosthetics like this continues to develop and advance, opening areas for mechanical engineers who are interested in the health field.

"We are on the precipice of huge advances in the field of robotics with the potential for new technology to become more deeply integrated into our every day lives."[29]

—Beth Marcus, senior principal technologist for Amazon Robotics

Computer Centric

In addition to the types of jobs available to mechanical engineers, how they do their jobs will continue to evolve. Mechanical engineering has always been a hands-on field with engineers designing and making prototypes. While this is still true, it has also become a computer-centric field. Today, mechanical engineers extensively use analysis software to help them determine the best process to use when manufacturing products and using machines. When it comes to design, mechanical engineers

Printing Predictions

3-D printing is becoming part of manufacturing around the world, and professionals foresee increased adoption in the next decade. For mechanical engineers, certain prototypes and components can be created with 3-D printers. One of the latest technologies is the Metal X 3-D printer, which prints rods of metal powder bound together with thermoplastic that mechanical engineers can use to produce prototypes. Greg Mark, CEO of Markforged, believes that metal printing is fast becoming a viable option for mainstream designers and engineers. "Mechanical engineers are going to become considerably more efficient," he says. "There are 2 million mechanical engineers who can design a part in hours, but have been waiting four to six weeks to get that part out of metal. They're about to have next-day access, accelerating innovation."

Quoted in Michael Molitch-Hou, "3D Printing Predictions for 2018: Industry Leaders Weigh In," Engineering.com, December 27, 2017. www.engineering.com.

must understand how to use the latest CAD tools, which are continually advancing. Additionally, increasing numbers of tools and machines in manufacturing are computer based, so mechanical engineers must understand how to use these systems. And, as manufacturing becomes more automated with robotics, mechanical engineers must be able to understand how to use and work with the robotics in the manufacturing processes.

Who Will Do Best?

With increased focus on technology, the environment, and automation, mechanical engineers who are both flexible and able to learn and obtain new skills throughout their careers will have the greatest chance of obtaining mechanical engineering jobs and moving up the career ladder. Patrick Kniveton, president of the Institution of Mechanical Engineers, writes:

As an engineer, I have always expected to challenge, to question,
and to find better ways of doing
things. I grit my teeth when I hear
phrases like "the science is settled."
That should be heresy to our profession, and not the way we should
think. Man's progress would stall if
we all thought that way. Engineers should look forward;
find the next step, the new idea, and the next innovation.[30]

"Engineers should look forward; find the next step, the new idea, and the next innovation."[30]

—Patrick Kniveton, president of the Institution of Mechanical Engineers

Those who do so will likely find themselves in a challenging, exciting, and forward-looking career.

CHAPTER 7

Interview with a Mechanical Engineer

Rick Brown has a bachelor of science in aerospace engineering and a master of science in mechanical engineering. He has worked as a mechanical engineer for twenty-seven years and has advanced to a supervisory nuclear engineer at the Norfolk Naval Shipyard. His group provides engineering services for the navy's nuclear-powered naval vessels. Brown says that one of the most important lessons he has learned during his career is the importance of being able to communicate. He discussed his career during an interview with the author.

Q: Why did you become a mechanical engineer?

A: For me, as a kid, when I saw machines I was really fascinated by them. My father was an agricultural major in college, and learned much about agriculture machines and the mechanics of them, which he taught me when I was young. We would take apart machines and put them back together. When it was time to go to college, I decided to apply for the engineering school at University of Virginia because of my interest in mechanics, and because I was good at math and science.

Q: Can you describe your typical workday?

A: What my group does is write procedures for taking apart the equipment and reactors of the navy vessels in order for repairs to be completed. When the procedures are being followed by the mechanics on deck, we are there to oversee them. Also, for part of our day, I do some equipment design for special tooling if certain tools are needed that we do not currently have for repairs. Other tasks include when equipment breaks, my group evaluates and writes instructions on how to repair the equipment for the mechanics.

Q: What do you like most about your job?

A: When I was a mechanical engineer, and not a supervisor, one of [the] things I have really liked was overseeing the operations on deck. I did this to ensure the instructions I wrote were working safely and correctly as they were being implemented by the mechanics on deck. The engineers who write the instructions are required to be on-site when the work is completed to ensure everything is safe. As a supervisor, the part of my job that I like is all the people I work with—from my team to the mechanics on deck doing the hands-on work.

Q: What do you like least about your job?

A: Earlier in my career, the hardest part of the job was shift work—working different shifts every few weeks, which included nights and weekend[s]. Also, initially, when I first started as an engineer, I did not like all of the reading and writing that I discovered the job included. However, I have become accustomed to that aspect of the job over the years.

Q: What personal qualities do you find most valuable for this type of engineering work?

A: Being able to communicate effectively and deal with people of all different backgrounds is essential to the job. Coming into the job with a solid understanding of mathematics and science is needed, and the ability to learn and understand what is specific to the job.

Q: What is the best way to prepare for this type of engineering job?

A: In high school, students should focus on math and science and obtain good grades in those subjects. Explore the different disciplines of engineering and see which interests you most before choosing one to major in at college. And don't forget the reading and writing, of course! Those who are effective at both math and verbal skills will have the best chance of doing well in this career.

Q: What special training did you need in your career?

A: Because of the aspect of our work with nuclear reactors, all the civilians who work on these, like myself, and the military receive special training by the navy, and receive certification. We are required to continue this education with classes so we can requalify throughout the years.

Q: What other advice do you have for students who might be interested in a career as a mechanical engineer?

A: Always think about what you want to do next. Learn that job before you even get it. If you want to be a supervisor, learn and understand what that job requires on your own. Additionally, learn how to make decisions and take risk assessment of different situations.

SOURCE NOTES

Introduction: Advancing Each Day

1. Quoted in Sue Shellenbarger, "Engineer Returns to Work After Years at Home with the Children," *Wall Street Journal*, May 3, 2016. www.wsj.com.
2. Marla Johnston, comment on CareerVillage, "Why Did You Want to Be a Mechanical Engineer?," May 11, 2016. www.careervillage.org.

Chapter 1: What Does a Mechanical Engineer Do?

3. Quoted in Kristen Lee, "Here's What It Takes to Build Cars That Run on the Fuel of the Future," Jalopnik, May 26, 2017. https://jalopnik.com.
4. Quoted in Benedict Bahner, "Mechanical Engineer Anya Lehrner Attains Dream Job as Roller Coaster Designer," American Society of Mechanical Engineers. www.asme.org.
5. Quoted in Brian Heater, "MIT's Cheetah 3 Robot Is Built to Save Lives," TechCrunch, July 7, 2017. https://techcrunch.com.
6. Quoted in Erica Giannini, "Engineering Spotlight: Meet Morgan!," *Sierra Blog*, March 20, 2015. www.sierrainstruments.com.
7. Marla Johnston, comment on CareerVillage, "What Do Mechanical Engineers Do on a Day-to-Day Basis?," February 11, 2016. www.careervillage.org.

Chapter 2: How Do You Become a Mechanical Engineer?

8. Quoted in Northeastern University, "First a Passion for Legos; Now a Sr. Mechanical Engineer," 2011. www.mie.neu.edu.
9. Quoted in Matt McKinney, "Aspiring Engineers, Artists and Doctors Help Drive Spike in Popularity of Norfolk Public Schools' Specialty Programs," *Virginian-Pilot* (Norfolk, VA), January 1, 2018. https://pilotonline.com.
10. BigFuture, "Major: Mechanical Engineering," 2018. https://bigfuture.collegeboard.org.

11. National Society of Professional Engineers, "Why Get Licensed?," 2018. www.nspc.org.
12. Quoted in EngineerJobs.com, "Is A Mechanical Engineering Master's Worth It?," January 5, 2015. https://magazine.engi neerjobs.com.

Chapter 3: What Skills and Personal Qualities Matter Most—and Why?

13. Quoted in Construction Forum St. Louis, "A Day in the Life of Mechanical Engineer, Lauren Blas," 2013. www.construct forstl.org.
14. Quoted in Eric Hanson, "The Real Life of a Mechanical Engineer: Scott Wertel on Being a Successful Consultant," Redshift, October 20, 2015. www.autodesk.com.
15. Quoted in Eric Newton, "Creativity as a Key to Engineering Innovation," LiveScience, August 31, 2012. www.livescience .com.
16. Quoted in Bright Knowledge, "My Job Explained: Assistant Mechanical Engineer," 2018. www.brightknowledge.org.
17. Quoted in Aspiring Mormon Women, "Career Day: Mechanical Engineering," July 7, 2013. http://aspiringmormonwomen .org.

Chapter 4: What Is It like to Work as a Mechanical Engineer?

18. Quoted in Construction Forum St. Louis, "A Day in the Life of Mechanical Engineer, Lauren Blas."
19. Quoted in Science Buddies, "Science Careers: Interview with Seng Chang." www.sciencebuddies.org.
20. Quoted in Aspiring Mormon Women, "Career Day."
21. Quoted in Institution of Mechanical Engineers, "Yassmin Abdel-Magied AMIMechE, Well Engineer, Shell," 2018. www .imeche.org.

Chapter 5: Advancement and Other Job Opportunities

22. Quoted in Auston Matta, "What Are Some Possibilities for Advancement or Promotions as a Mechanical Engineer?," Chron, 2018. work.chron.com.
23. Matta, "What Are Some Possibilities for Advancement or Promotions as a Mechanical Engineer?"
24. Heather Clarke, "My Job Explained: Engineering Business Operations Manager," Bright Knowledge. www.brightknowledge.org.
25. Michele Miller, "Dr. Michele Miller," Engineer Girl. https://www.engineergirl.org.
26. Subi Shah, "How to Start an Engineering Consultancy Firm of One," Redshift, August 11, 2015. www.autodesk.com.

Chapter 6: What Does the Future Hold for Mechanical Engineers?

27. Quoted in Randy Yagi, "Mechanical Engineers Have a Bright Future, Says San Francisco Professor," CBS San Francisco, September 22, 2014. http://sanfrancisco.cbslocal.com.
28. Nicholas Roche, "The Future of Electric Cars," CST Careers 2030, July 27, 2017. https://careers2030.cst.org.
29. Quoted in Kurt Schlosser, "Geek of the Week: Amazon Robotics' Beth Marcus Helps Machines and Humans Work Better Together," GeekWire, June 23, 2017. www.geekwire.com.
30. Patrick Kniveton, "Proud to Be an Engineer—the Future for Mechanical Engineers," Engineers Journal, March 27, 2014. www.engineersjournal.ie.

FIND OUT MORE

American Society of Mechanical Engineers (ASME)

www.asme.org

The ASME is a not-for-profit membership organization that provides a way for people to share knowledge about mechanical engineering, provides career development information, and has information about various engineering disciplines. The website provides information on the latest news in engineering, interviews with engineers, and information on certification.

EngineerGirl

National Academy of Engineering
500 Fifth St. NW
Washington, DC 20001
www.engineergirl.com

This website provides interviews with female engineers of all disciplines, and people can post questions to these engineers, who will answer. Additionally, it provides basic information on what engineers do, what types of careers are available, and the future potential for engineers.

Engineering.com

www.engineeering.com

This website provides over two thousand articles a year about engineering. It provides information on the latest projects and advances in all engineering disciplines. The website also offers career advice for current and aspiring engineers.

National Society of Professional Engineers

1420 King St.

Alexandria, VA 22314

www.nspe.org

The National Society of Professional Engineers is a national organization providing information for those certified as Professional Engineers. Its website provides specific information for engineering students, online courses and articles about the industry, and information on how to get certification.

Society of Women Engineers

130 E. Randolph St., Suite 3500

Chicago, IL 60602

https://societyofwomenengineers.swe.org

The Society of Women Engineers is an organization of women engineers that provides a place and way for them to share their ideas and achievements in the engineering industry. The website provides articles on STEM initiatives in schools, scholarship information for aspiring female engineering majors, and an online magazine.

PICTURE CREDITS

cover: Dan Howell/Shutterstock.com

 6: Maury Aaseng

11: Suwin/Shutterstock.com

18: science photo/Shutterstock.com

37: nd3000/Shutterstock.com

44: Associated Press

Leanne Currie-McGhee is the author of several educational books and has an electrical engineering degree. She lives in Norfolk, Virginia, with her husband, Keith, and daughters, Grace and Hope.